VOL. 136

HAL•LEONARD

GUITAR PLAY-ALONG

Guitar THEMES

T0081934

ISBN 978-1-61780-437-3

HAL•LEONARD®
CORPORATION

7777 W. BLUEMOUND RD. P.O. BOX 13819 MILWAUKEE, WI 53213

Visit Hal Leonard Online at
www.halleonard.com

CONTENTS

Page	Title	Demo Track	Play-Along Track
6	Theme from E.T. (The Extra-Terrestrial) JOHN WILLIAMS	1	2
22	The Godfather (Love Theme) SLASH	3	4
26	He's a Pirate KLAUS BADELT	5	6
13	Linus and Lucy GARY HOEY	7	8
30	Misirlou DICK DALE	9	10
36	Peter Gunn DUANE EDDY	11	12
38	(Ghost) Riders in the Sky (A Cowboy Legend) THE RAMRODS	13	14
44	Theme from Spider Man ROBERT J. HARRIS & PAUL FRANCIS WEBSTER	15	16
	TUNING NOTES	17	

Guitar Notation Legend

THE MUSICAL STAFF shows pitches and rhythms and is divided by bar lines into measures. Pitches are named after the first seven letters of the alphabet.

TABLATURE graphically represents the guitar fingerboard. Each horizontal line represents a string, and each number represents a fret.

4th string, 2nd fret

1st & 2nd strings open, played together

open D chord

HALF-STEP BEND: Strike the note and bend up 1/2 step.

WHOLE-STEP BEND: Strike the note and bend up one step.

GRACE NOTE BEND: Strike the note and immediately bend up as indicated.

SLIGHT (MICROTONE) BEND: Strike the note and bend up 1/4 step.

BEND AND RELEASE: Strike the note and bend up as indicated, then release back to the original note. Only the first note is struck.

PRE-BEND: Bend the note as indicated, then strike it.

VIBRATO: The string is vibrated by rapidly bending and releasing the note with the fretting hand.

PALM MUTING: The note is partially muted by the pick hand lightly touching the string(s) just before the bridge.

HAMMER-ON: Strike the first (lower) note with one finger, then sound the higher note (on the same string) with another finger by fretting it without picking.

PULL-OFF: Place both fingers on the notes to be sounded. Strike the first note and without picking, pull the finger off to sound the second (lower) note.

LEGATO SLIDE: Strike the first note and then slide the same fret-hand finger up or down to the second note. The second note is not struck.

SHIFT SLIDE: Same as legato slide, except the second note is struck.

TRILL: Very rapidly alternate between the notes indicated by continuously hammering on and pulling off.

TAPPING: Hammer ("tap") the fret indicated with the pick-hand index or middle finger and pull off to the note fretted by the fret hand.

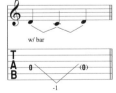

NATURAL HARMONIC: Strike the note while the fret-hand lightly touches the string directly over the fret indicated.

PINCH HARMONIC: The note is fretted normally and a harmonic is produced by adding the edge of the thumb or the tip of the index finger of the pick hand to the normal pick attack.

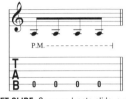

TREMOLO PICKING: The note is picked as rapidly and continuously as possible.

VIBRATO BAR DIVE AND RETURN: The pitch of the note or chord is dropped a specified number of steps (in rhythm), then returned to the original pitch.

VIBRATO BAR SCOOP: Depress the bar just before striking the note, then quickly release the bar.

VIBRATO BAR DIP: Strike the note and then immediately drop a specified number of steps, then release back to the original pitch.

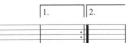

Additional Musical Definitions

 (accent)
- Accentuate note (play it louder).

 (staccato)
- Play the note short.

D.S. al Coda
- Go back to the sign (%), then play until the measure marked "***To Coda***," then skip to the section labelled "**Coda**."

D.C. al Fine
- Go back to the beginning of the song and play until the measure marked "***Fine***" (end).

Fill

N.C.

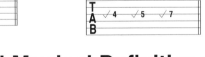

- Label used to identify a brief melodic figure which is to be inserted into the arrangement.

- Harmony is implied.

- Repeat measures between signs.

- When a repeated section has different endings, play the first ending only the first time and the second ending only the second time.

Theme from E.T.
(The Extra-Terrestrial)

from the Universal Picture E.T. (THE EXTRA-TERRESTRIAL)

Music by John Williams

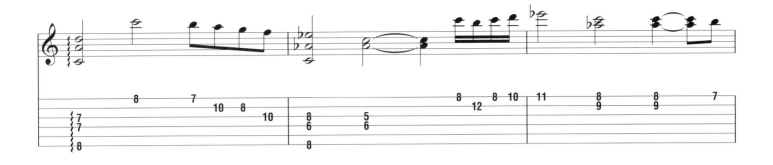

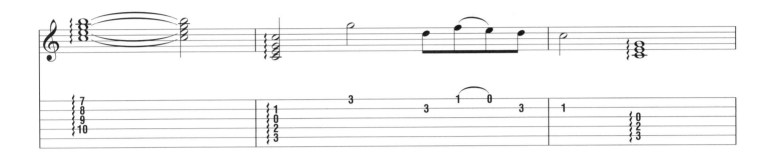

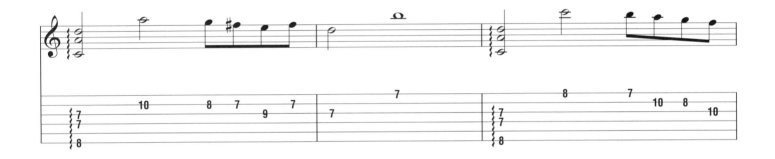

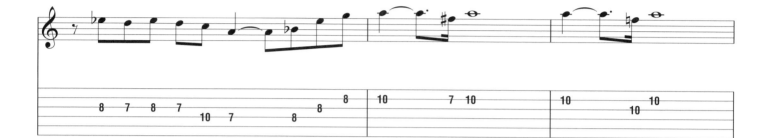

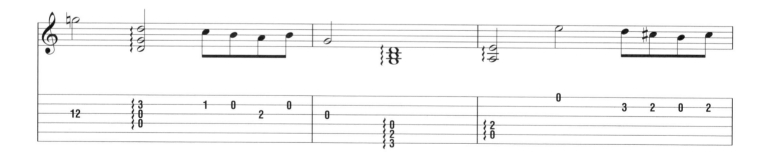

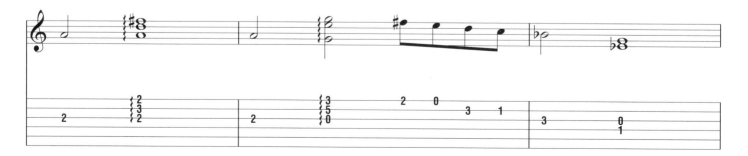

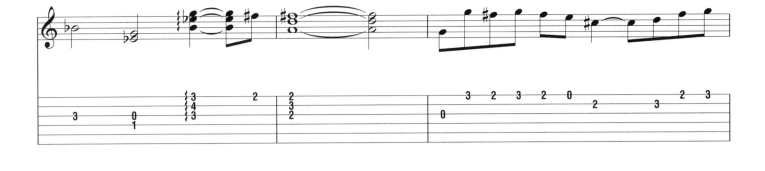

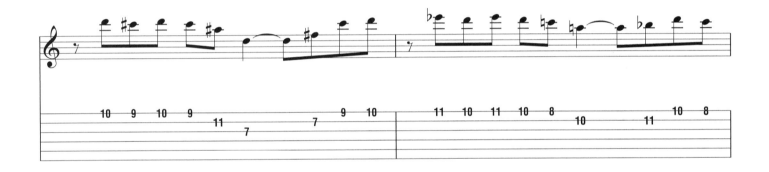

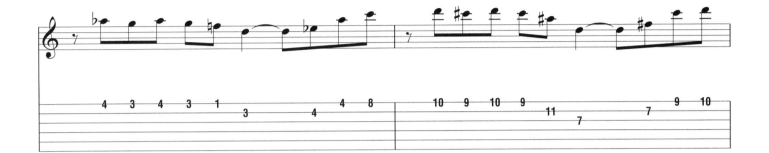

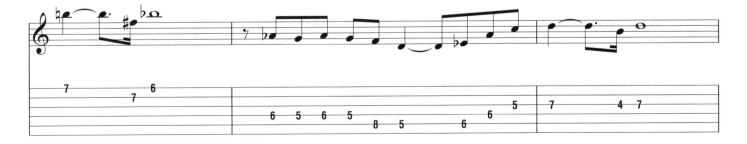

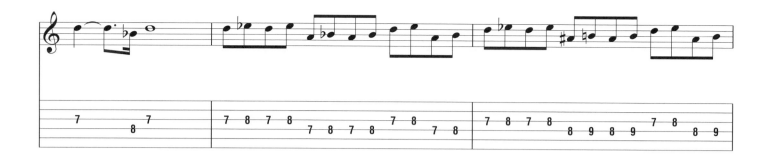

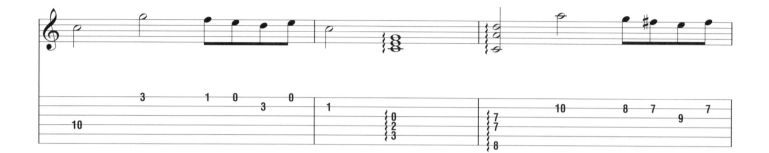

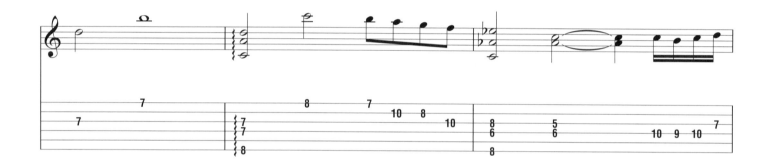

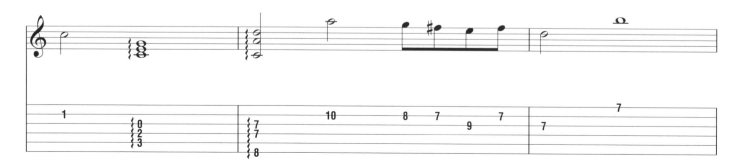

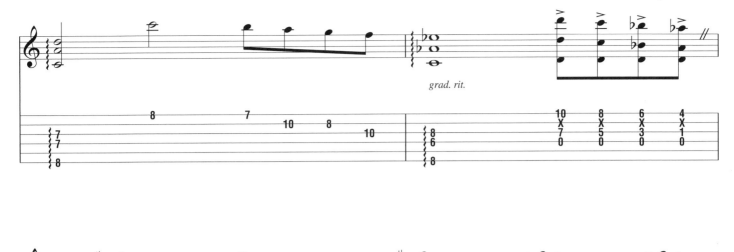

grad. rit.

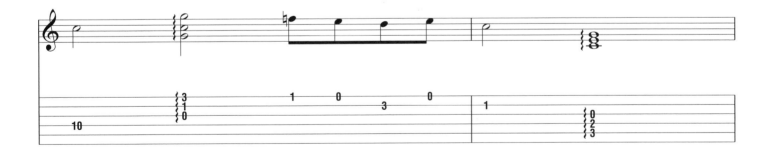

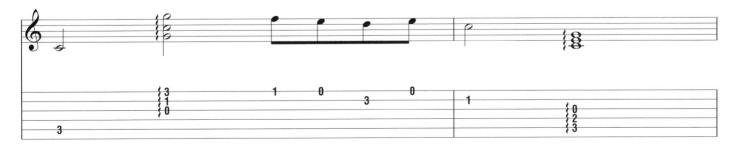

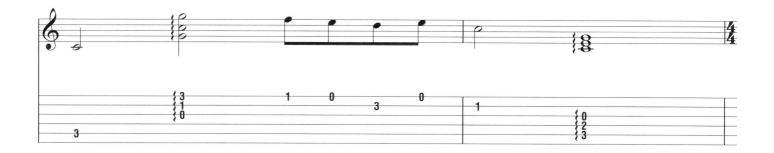

Quickly

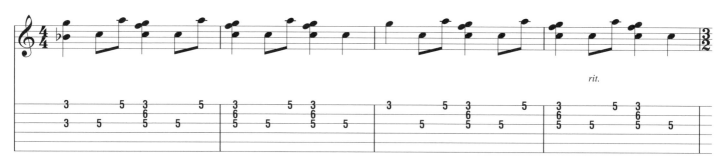

rit.

Largamente

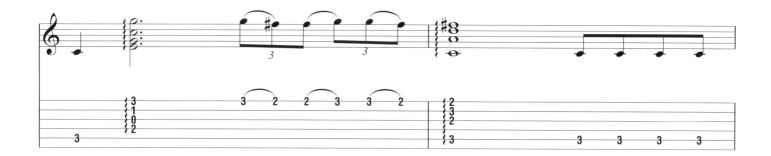

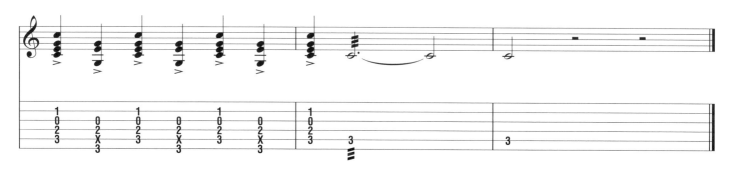

Linus and Lucy

By Vince Guaraldi

Tune down 1/2 step:
(low to high) E♭-A♭-D♭-G♭-B♭-E♭

Moderately fast ♩ = 162
Half-time feel

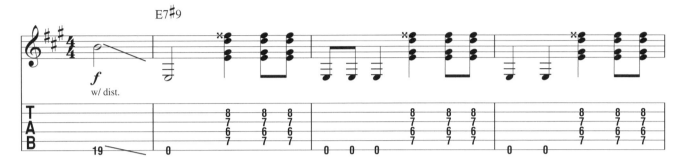

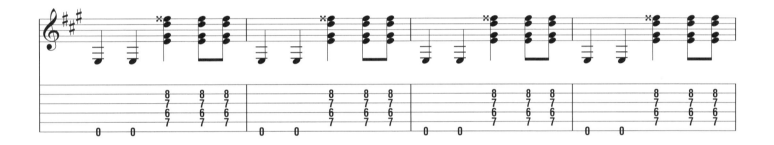

End half-time feel

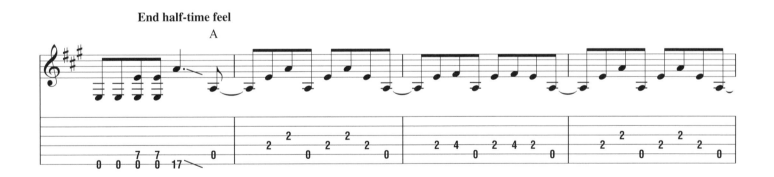

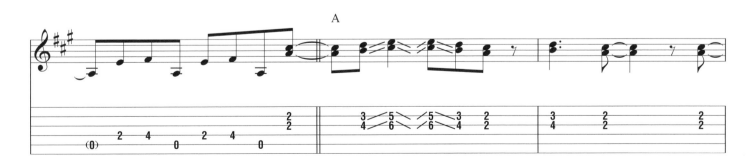

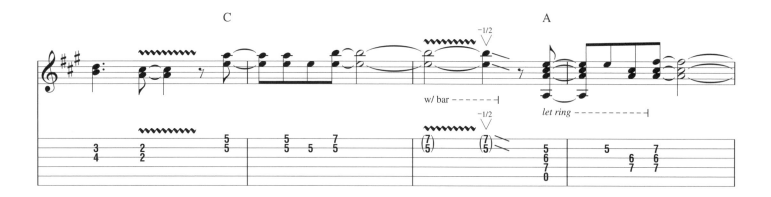

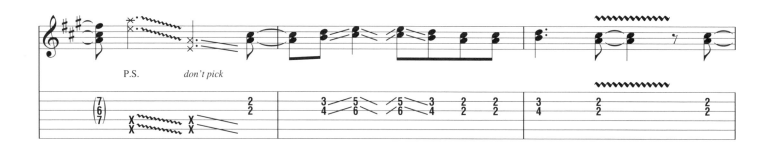

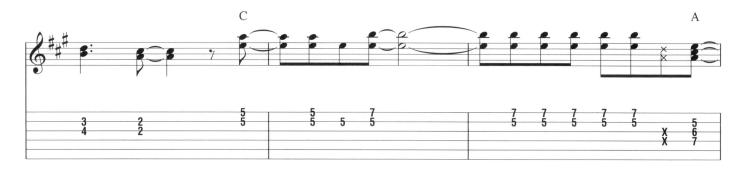

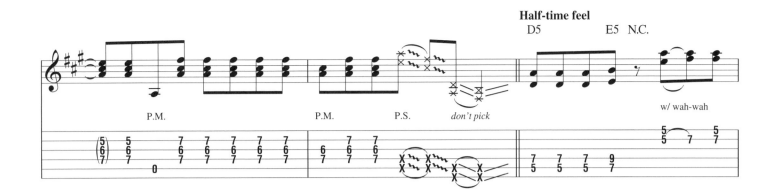

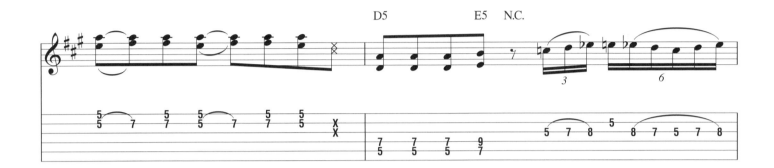

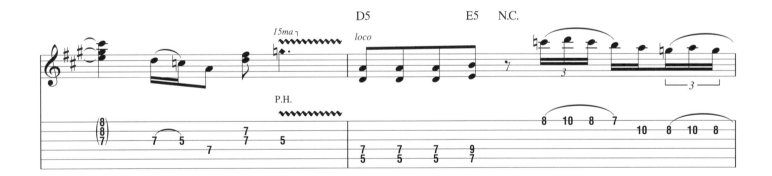

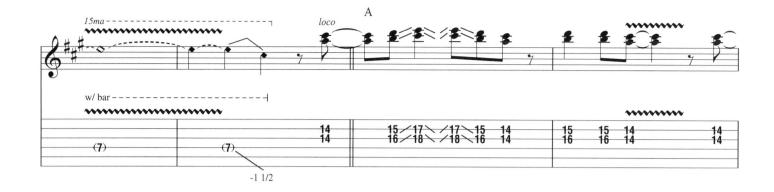

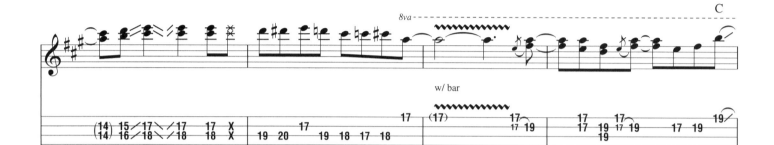

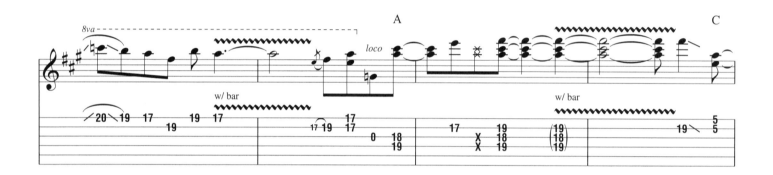

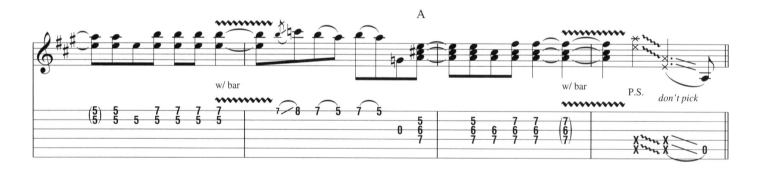

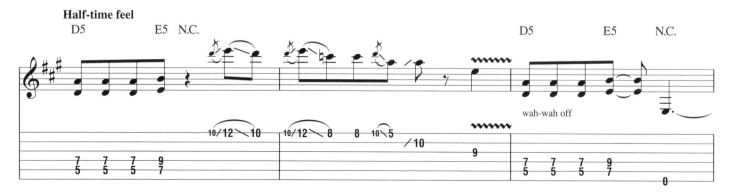

End half-time feel

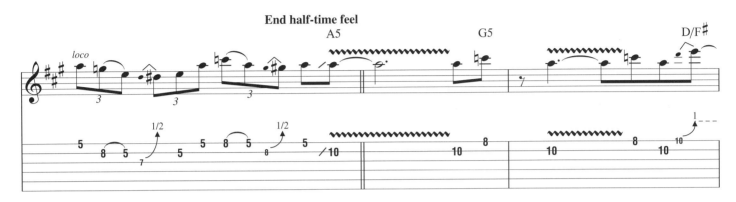

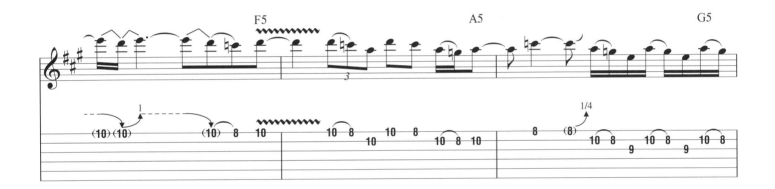

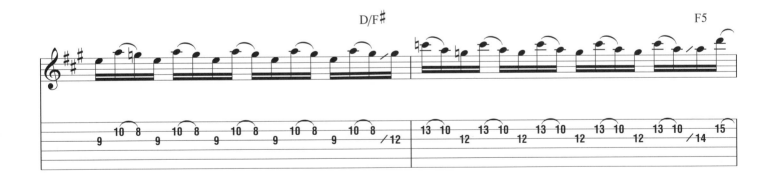

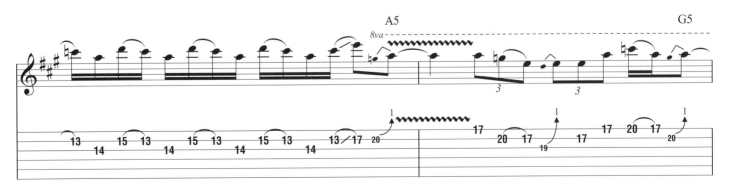

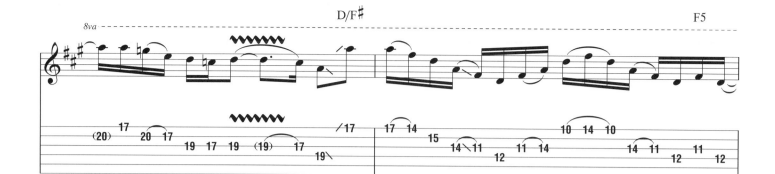

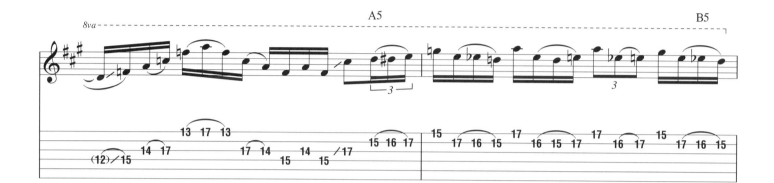

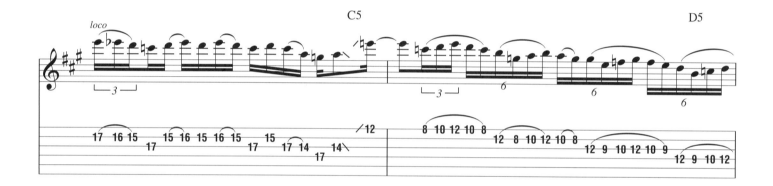

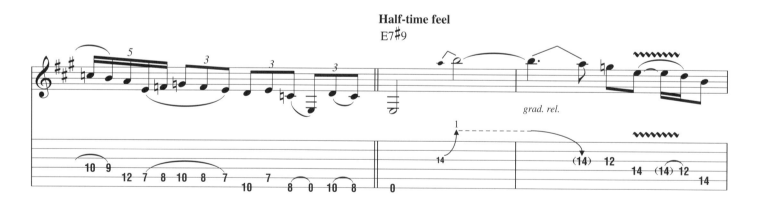

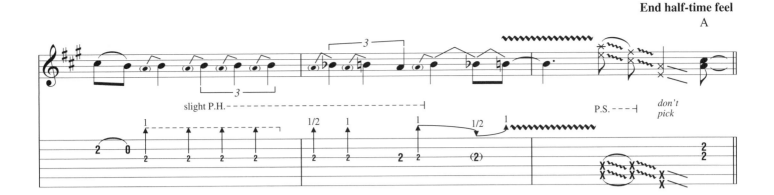

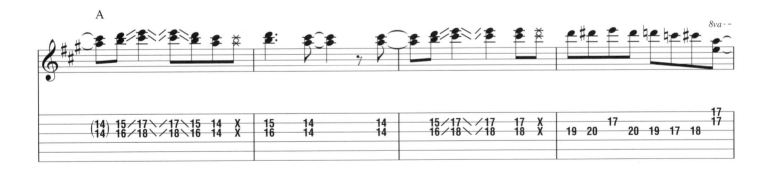

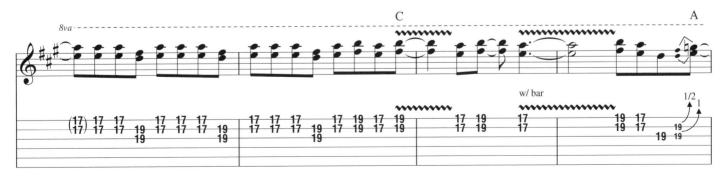

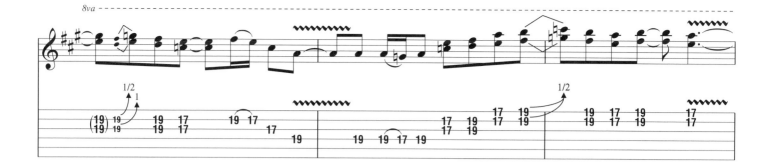

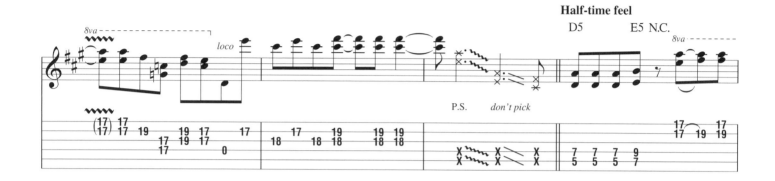

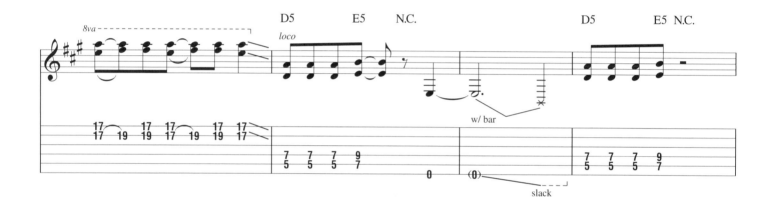

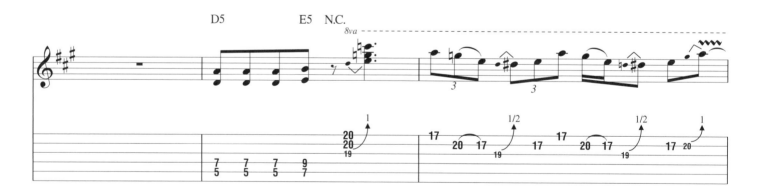

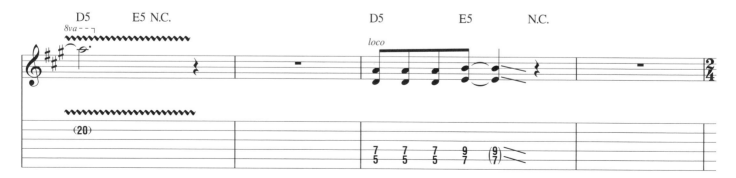

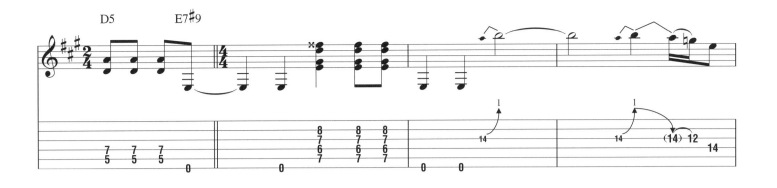

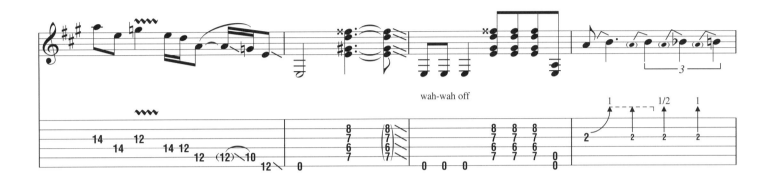

Free time

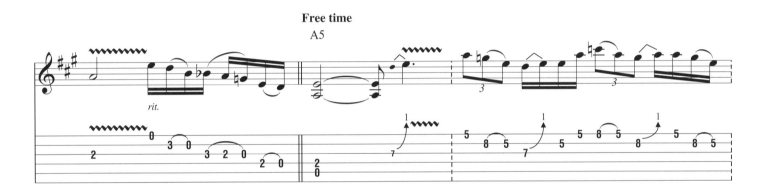

The Godfather (Love Theme)

from the Paramount Picture THE GODFATHER

By Nino Rota

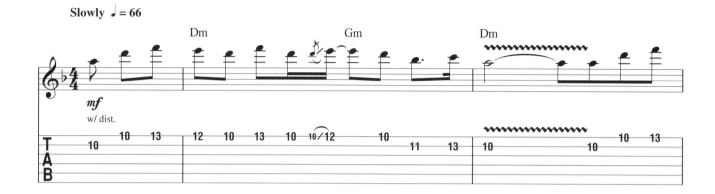

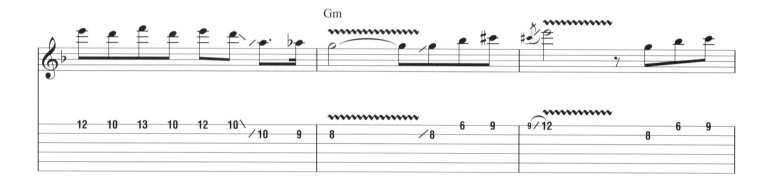

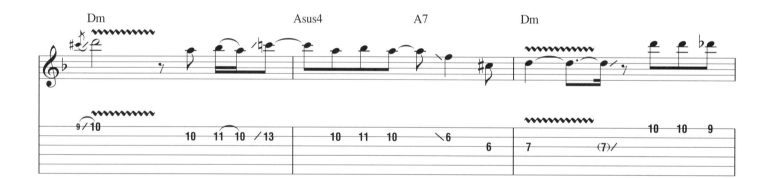

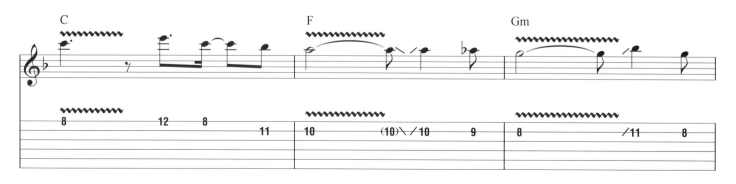

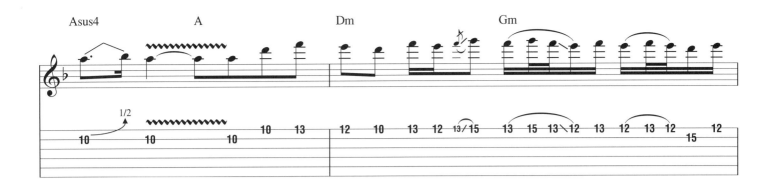

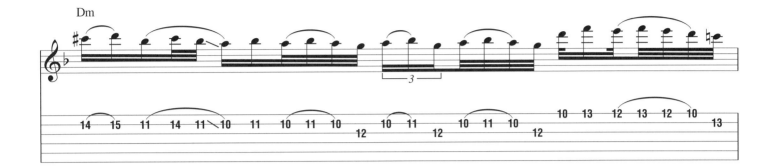

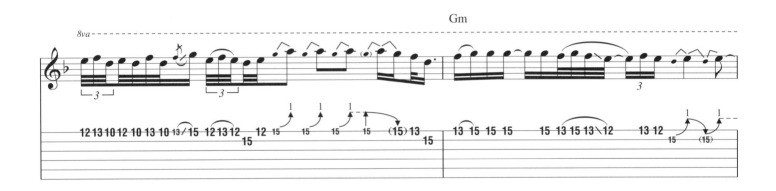

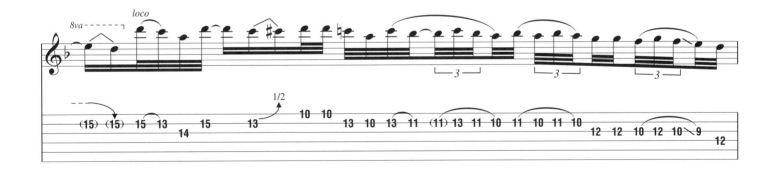

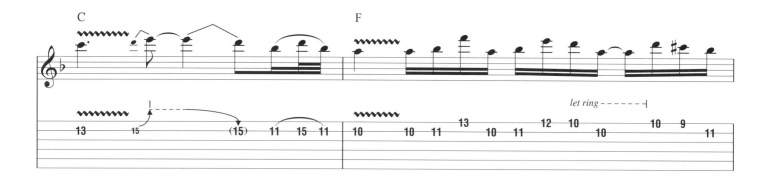

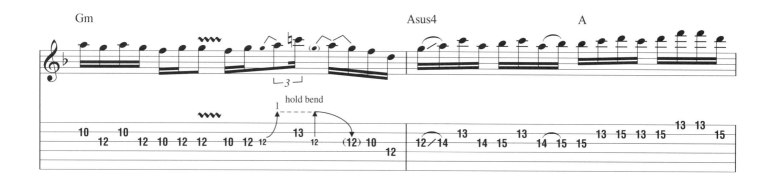

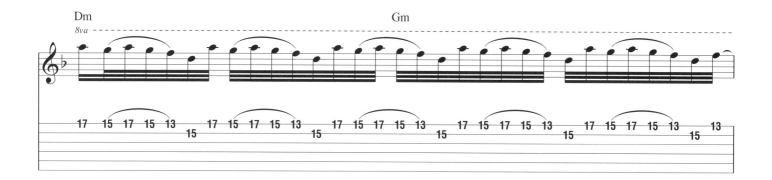

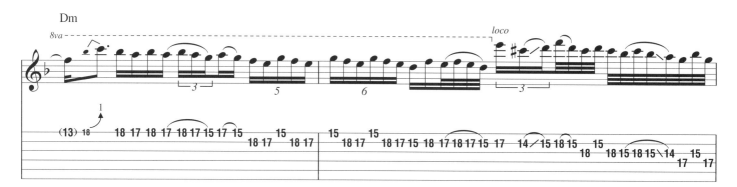

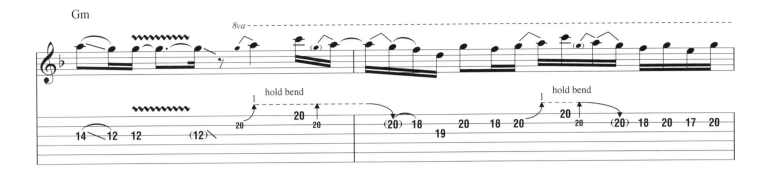

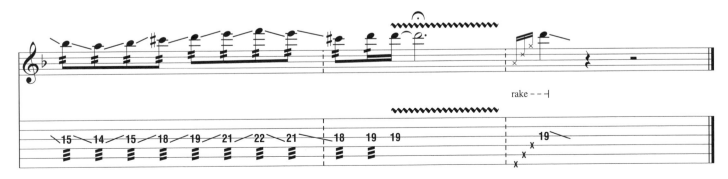

He's a Pirate

from Walt Disney Pictures' PIRATES OF THE CARIBBEAN: THE CURSE OF THE BLACK PEARL

Music by Klaus Badelt

Driving, in 4

Moderately fast, in 3

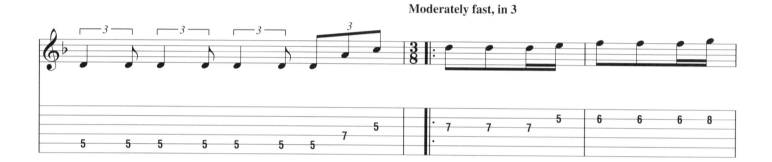

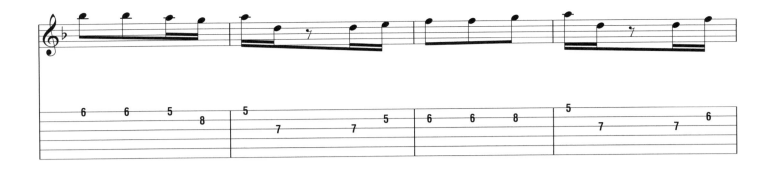

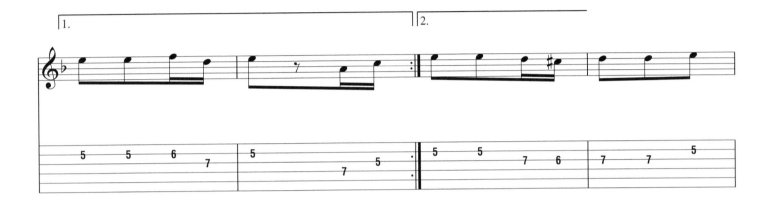

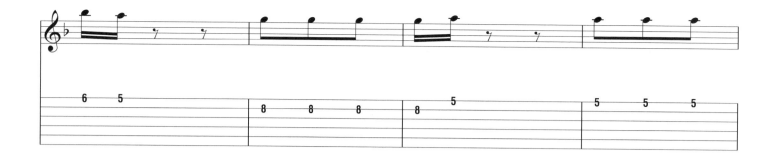

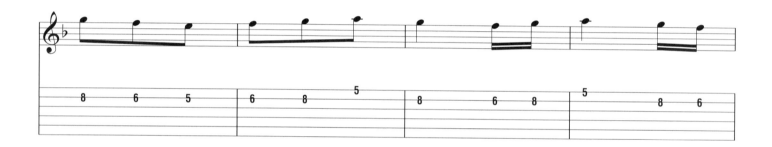

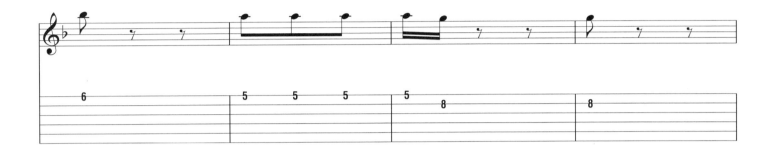

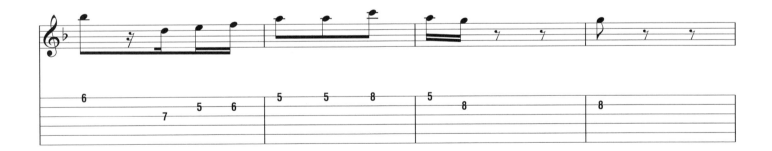

Misirlou

By Nicolas Roubanis

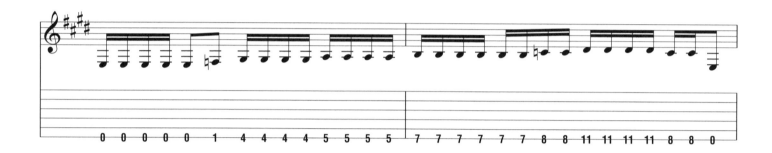

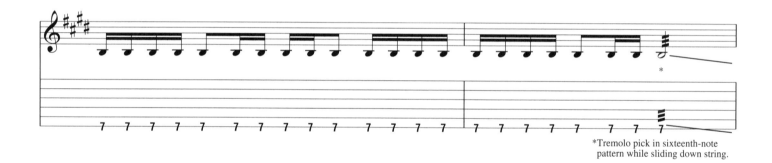

*Tremolo pick in sixteenth-note
pattern while sliding down string.

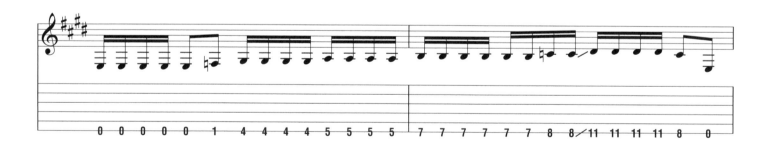

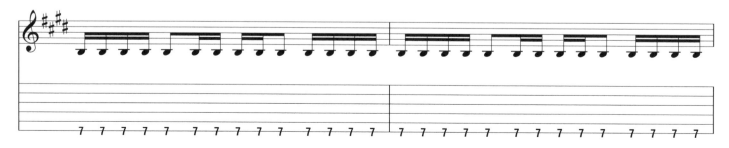

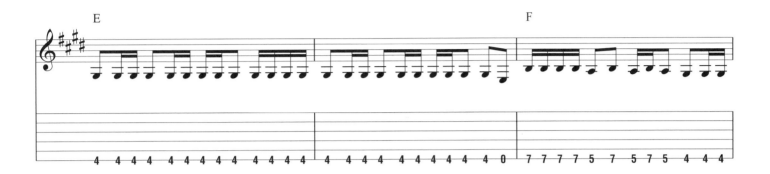

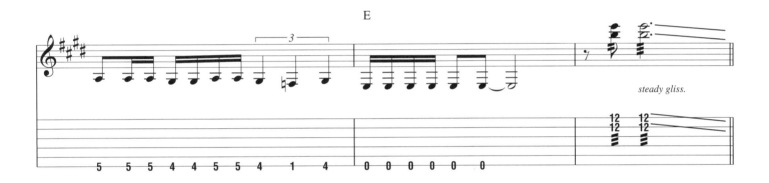

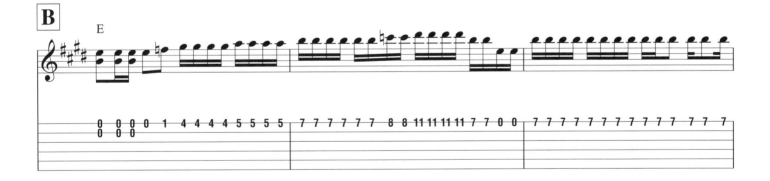

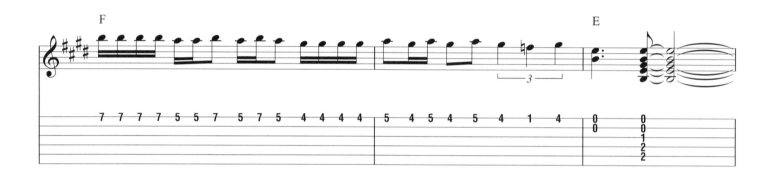

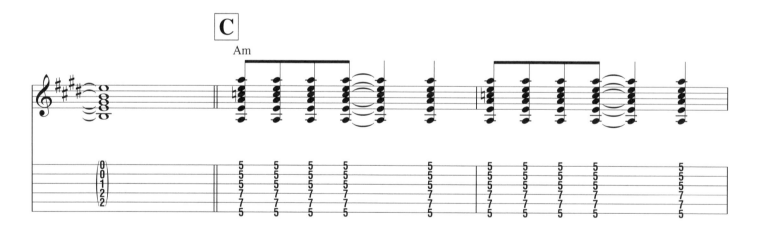

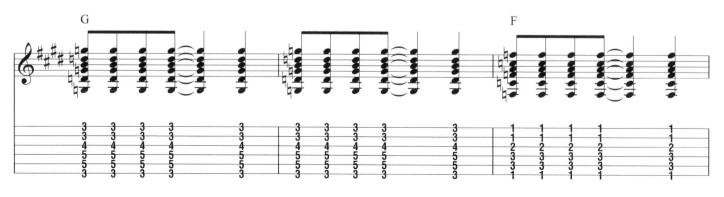

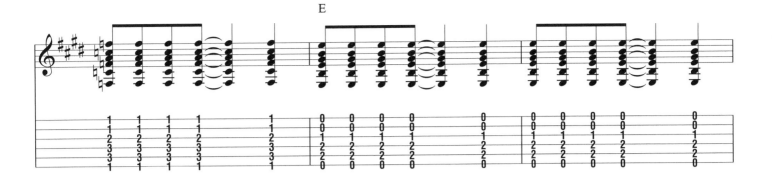

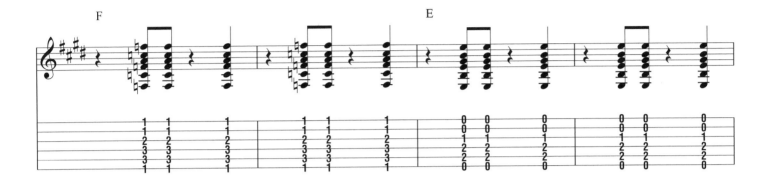

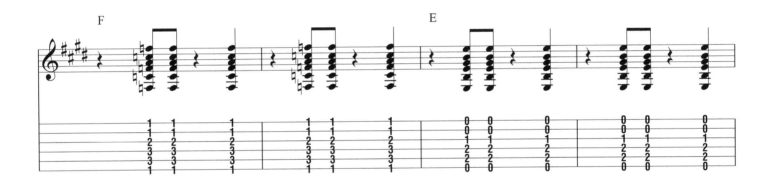

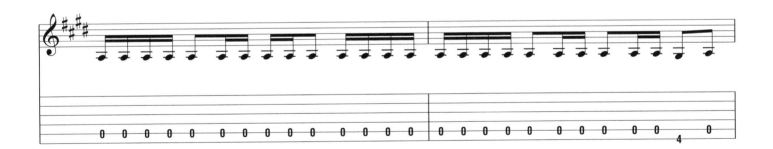

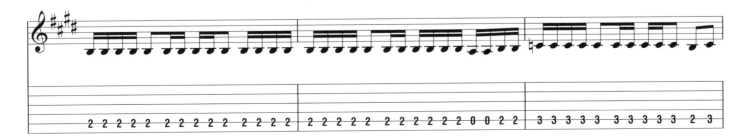

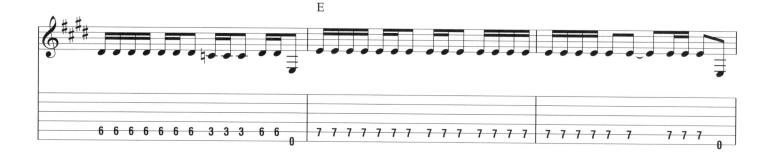

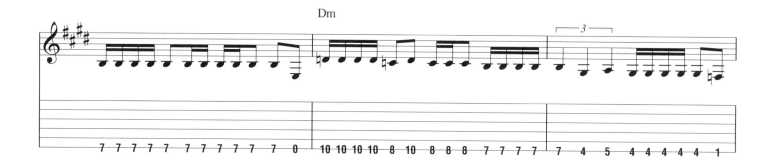

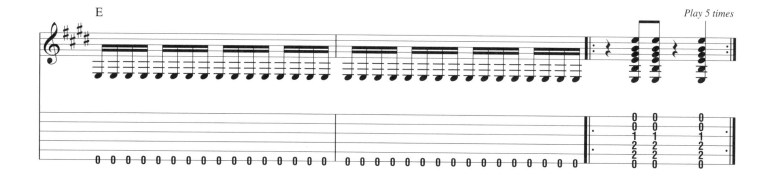

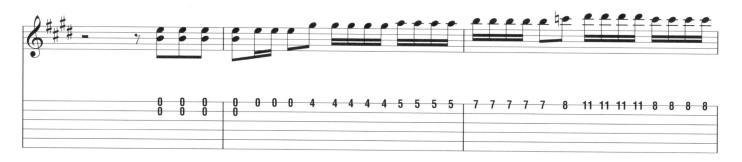

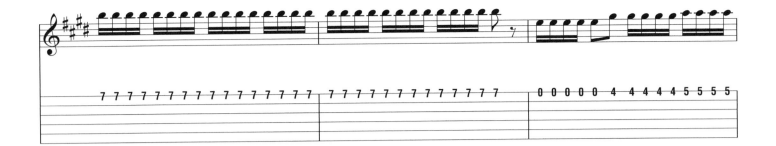

Repeat and fade

Peter Gunn

Theme Song from The Television Series
By Henry Mancini

Tune up 1/2 step:
(low to high) F-B♭-E♭-A♭-C-F

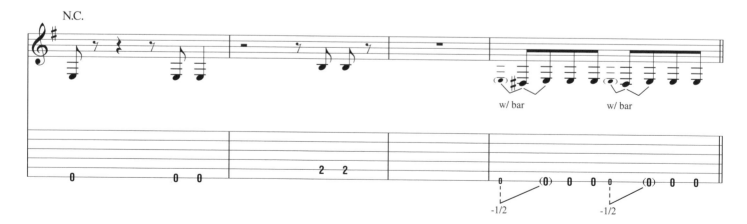

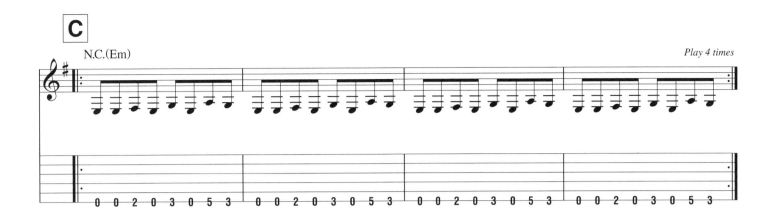

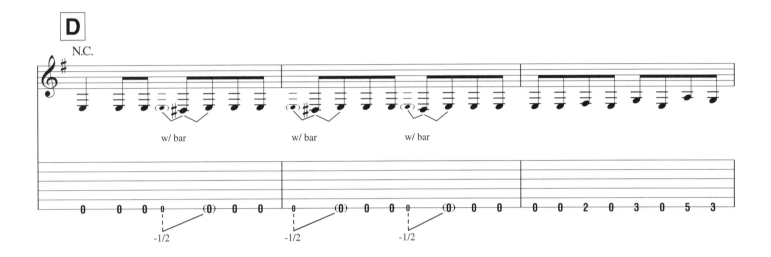

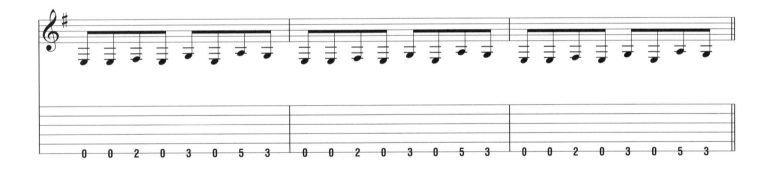

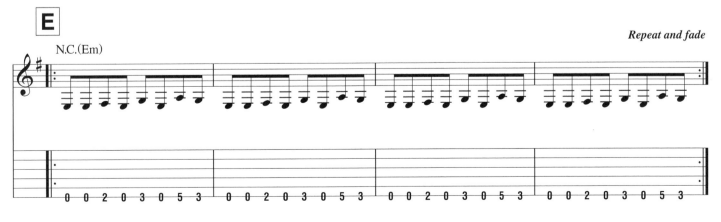

(Ghost) Riders in the Sky

(A Cowboy Legend)

from RIDERS IN THE SKY

By Stan Jones

Moderately ♩ = 114

N.C.

mf

w/ clean tone, slapback delay & amp tremolo

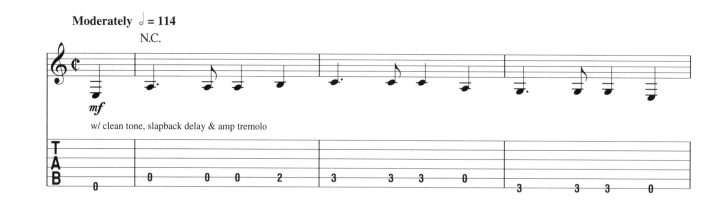

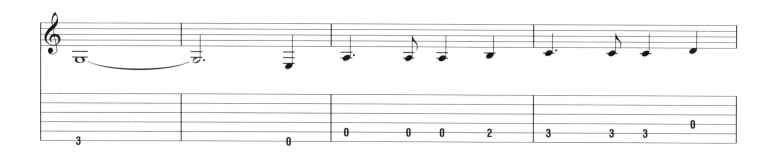

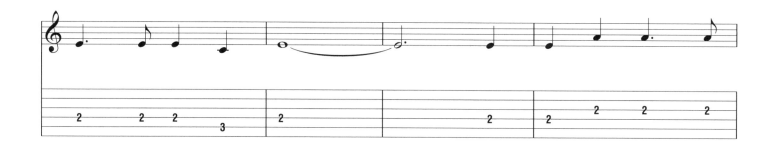

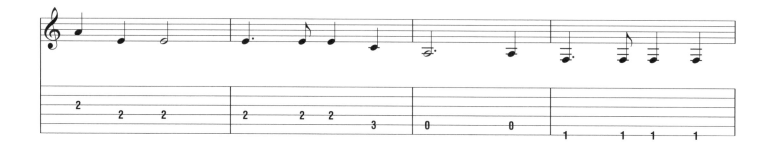

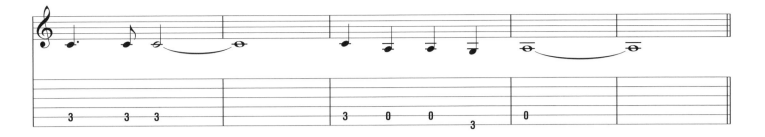

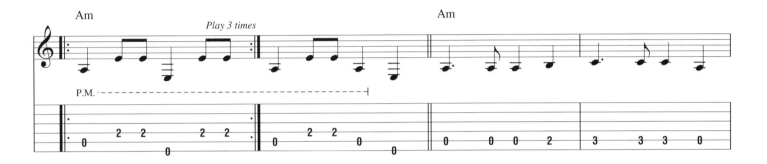

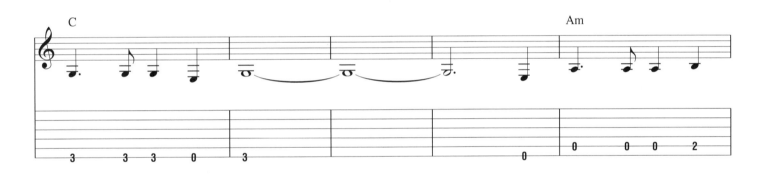

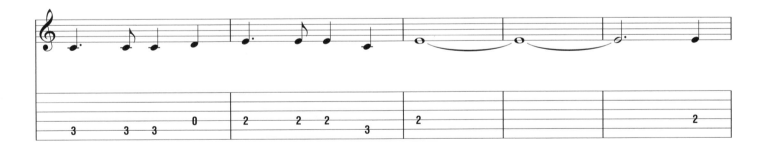

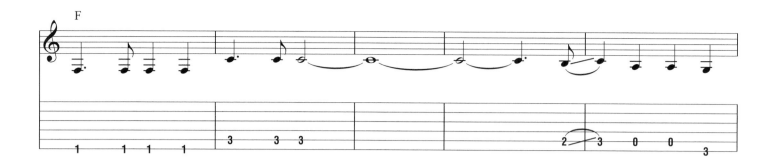

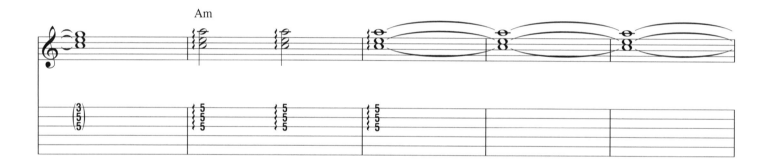

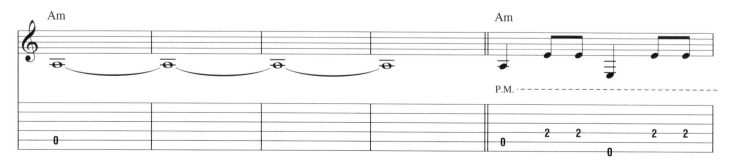

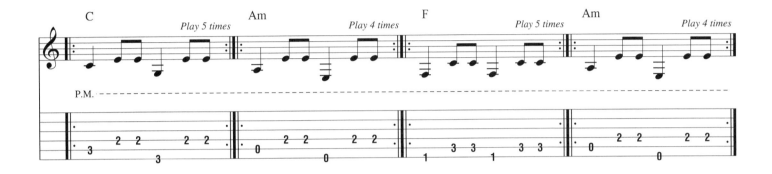

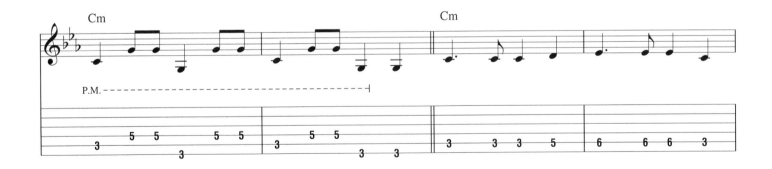

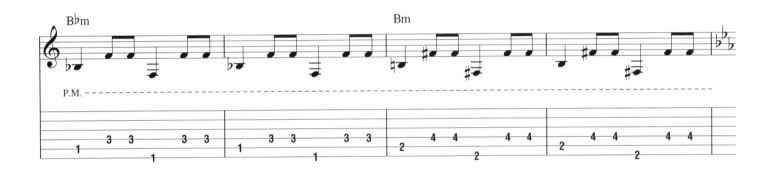

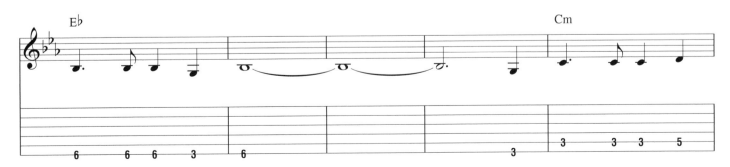

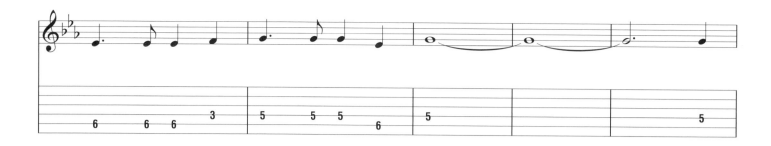

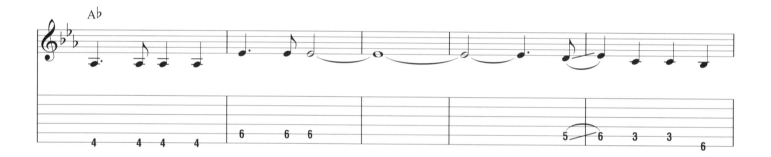

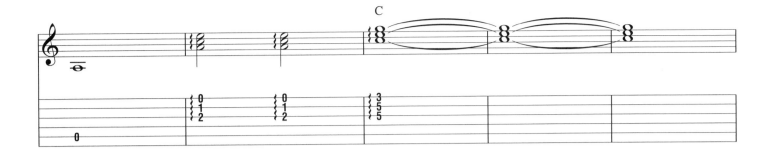

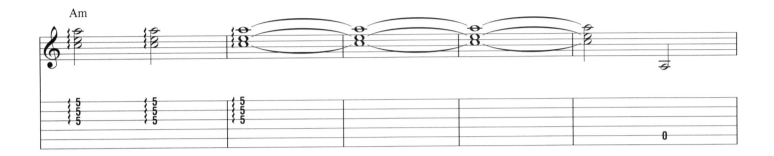

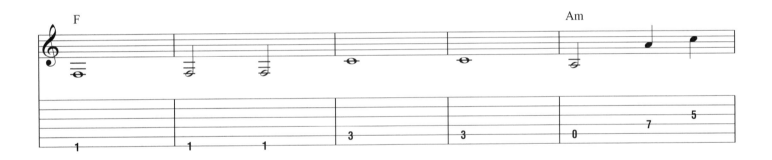

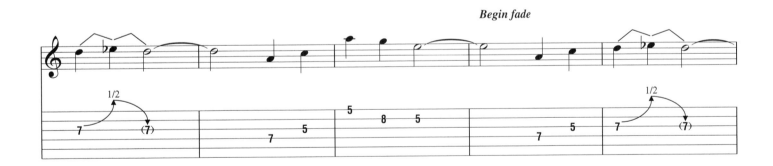

Theme from Spider Man

Written by Bob Harris and Paul Francis Webster

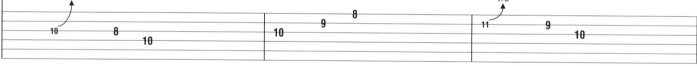

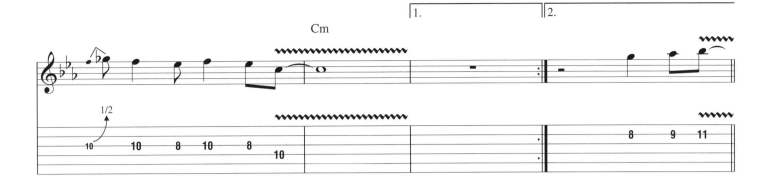

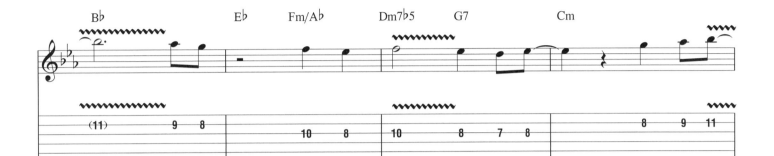

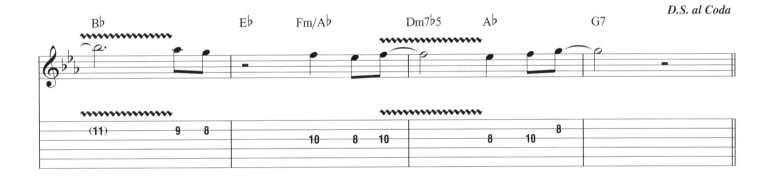

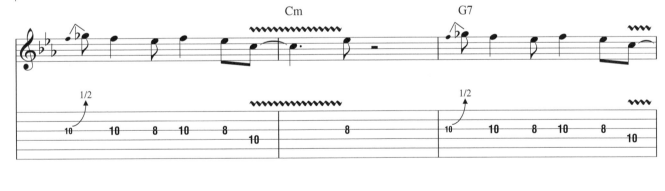

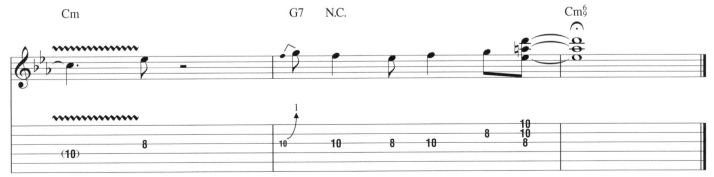

Hal•Leonard GUITAR PLAY-ALONG

INCLUDES TAB

This series will help you play your favorite songs quickly and easily. Just follow the tab and listen to the CD to hear how the guitar should sound, and then play along using the separate backing tracks. Mac or PC users can also slow down the tempo without changing pitch by using the CD in their computer. The melody and lyrics are included in the book so that you can sing or simply follow along.

1. ROCK 00699570 ....$16.99	**16. JAZZ** 00699584.............................$15.95	**31. CHRISTMAS HITS** 00699652.............................$14.95	**46. MAINSTREAM ROCK** 00699722.............................$16.95
2. ACOUSTIC 00699569.............................$16.95	**17. COUNTRY** 00699588.............................$15.95	**32. THE OFFSPRING** 00699653.............................$14.95	**47. HENDRIX SMASH HITS** 00699723.............................$19.95
3. HARD ROCK 00699573.............................$16.95	**18. ACOUSTIC ROCK** 00699577.............................$15.95	**33. ACOUSTIC CLASSICS** 00699656.............................$16.95	**48. AEROSMITH CLASSICS** 00699724.............................$17.99
4. POP/ROCK 00699571.............................$16.99	**19. SOUL** 00699578.............................$14.95	**34. CLASSIC ROCK** 00699658.............................$16.95	**49. STEVIE RAY VAUGHAN** 00699725.............................$16.95
5. MODERN ROCK 00699574 ....$16.99	**20. ROCKABILLY** 00699580.............................$14.95	**35. HAIR METAL** 00699660.............................$16.95	**50. 2000s METAL** 00699726.............................$14.95
6. '90s ROCK 00699572.............................$16.99	**21. YULETIDE** 00699602.............................$14.95	**36. SOUTHERN ROCK** 00699661.............................$16.95	**51. ALTERNATIVE '90s** 00699727.............................$12.95
7. BLUES 00699575.............................$16.95	**22. CHRISTMAS** 00699600.............................$15.95	**37. ACOUSTIC METAL** 00699662.............................$16.95	**52. FUNK** 00699728.............................$14.95
8. ROCK 00699585.............................$14.99	**23. SURF** 00699635.............................$14.95	**38. BLUES** 00699663.............................$16.95	**53. DISCO** 00699729.............................$14.99
9. PUNK ROCK 00699576.............................$14.95	**24. ERIC CLAPTON** 00699649.............................$17.99	**39. '80s METAL** 00699664.............................$16.99	**54. HEAVY METAL** 00699730.............................$14.95
10. ACOUSTIC 00699586.............................$16.95	**25. LENNON & McCARTNEY** 00699642 ....$16.99	**40. INCUBUS** 00699668.............................$17.95	**55. POP METAL** 00699731.............................$14.95
11. EARLY ROCK 0699579.............................$14.95	**26. ELVIS PRESLEY** 00699643.............................$14.95	**41. ERIC CLAPTON** 00699669.............................$16.95	**56. FOO FIGHTERS** 00699749.............................$14.95
12. POP/ROCK 00699587.............................$14.95	**27. DAVID LEE ROTH** 00699645.............................$16.95	**42. 2000s ROCK** 00699670.............................$16.99	**57. SYSTEM OF A DOWN** 00699751.............................$14.95
13. FOLK ROCK 00699581.............................$14.95	**28. GREG KOCH** 00699646.............................$14.95	**43. LYNYRD SKYNYRD** 00699681.............................$17.95	**58. BLINK-182** 00699772.............................$14.95
14. BLUES ROCK 00699582.............................$16.95	**29. BOB SEGER** 00699647.............................$14.95	**44. JAZZ** 00699689.............................$14.95	**59. GODSMACK** 00699773.............................$14.95
15. R&B 00699583.............................$14.95	**30. KISS** 00699644.............................$16.99	**45. TV THEMES** 00699718.............................$14.95	**60. 3 DOORS DOWN** 00699774.............................$14.95

61. SLIPKNOT
00699775......................$14.95

62. CHRISTMAS CAROLS
00699798......................$12.95

63. CREEDENCE CLEARWATER REVIVAL
00699802......................$16.99

64. OZZY OSBOURNE
00699803......................$16.99

65. THE DOORS
00699806......................$16.99

66. THE ROLLING STONES
00699807......................$16.95

67. BLACK SABBATH
00699808......................$16.99

**68. PINK FLOYD –
DARK SIDE OF THE MOON**
00699809......................$16.99

69. ACOUSTIC FAVORITES
00699810......................$14.95

70. OZZY OSBOURNE
00699805 ....$16.99

71. CHRISTIAN ROCK
00699824......................$14.95

72. ACOUSTIC '90s
00699827......................$14.95

73. BLUESY ROCK
00699829 ....$16.99

74. PAUL BALOCHE
00699831......................$14.95

75. TOM PETTY
00699882......................$16.99

76. COUNTRY HITS
00699884......................$14.95

77. BLUEGRASS
00699910......................$12.99

78. NIRVANA
00700132......................$16.99

88. ACOUSTIC ANTHOLOGY
00700175......................$19.95

81. ROCK ANTHOLOGY
00700176......................$22.99

82. EASY ROCK SONGS
00700177......................$12.99

83. THREE CHORD SONGS
00700178......................$16.99

84. STEELY DAN
00700200 ....$16.99

85. THE POLICE
00700269......................$16.99

86. BOSTON
00700465......................$16.99

87. ACOUSTIC WOMEN
00700763......................$14.99

88. GRUNGE
00700467 ....$16.99

91. BLUES INSTRUMENTALS
00700505 ....$14.99

**92. EARLY ROCK
INSTRUMENTALS**
00700506 ....$12.99

93. ROCK INSTRUMENTALS
00700507 ....$16.99

96. THIRD DAY
00700560......................$14.95

97. ROCK BAND
00700703......................$14.99

98. ROCK BAND
00700704......................$14.95

99. ZZ TOP
00700762 ....$16.99

100. B.B. KING
00700466 ....$14.99

102. CLASSIC PUNK
00700769......................$14.99

103. SWITCHFOOT
00700773......................$16.99

104. DUANE ALLMAN
00700846......................$16.99

106. WEEZER
00700958 ....$14.99

107. CREAM
00701069......................$16.99

108. THE WHO
00701053......................$16.99

109. STEVE MILLER
00701054......................$14.99

111. JOHN MELLENCAMP
00701056 ....$14.99

113. JIM CROCE
00701058 ....$14.99

114. BON JOVI
00701060 ....$14.99

115. JOHNNY CASH
00701070......................$16.99

116. THE VENTURES
00701124 ....$14.99

119. AC/DC CLASSICS
00701356 ....$17.99

120. PROGRESSIVE ROCK
00701457......................$14.99

122. CROSBY, STILLS & NASH
00701610......................$16.99

**123. LENNON & McCARTNEY
ACOUSTIC**
00701614......................$16.99

124. MODERN WORSHIP
00701629......................$14.99

126. BOB MARLEY
00701701......................$16.99

127. 1970s ROCK
00701739......................$14.99

128. 1960s ROCK
00701740......................$14.99

129. MEGADETH
00701741......................$14.99

130. IRON MAIDEN
00701742......................$14.99

131. 1990s ROCK
00701743......................$14.99

133. TAYLOR SWIFT
00701894......................$16.99

FOR MORE INFORMATION, SEE YOUR LOCAL MUSIC DEALER,
OR WRITE TO:

HAL•LEONARD®
CORPORATION
7777 W. BLUEMOUND RD. P.O. BOX 13819 MILWAUKEE, WI 53213

**For complete songlists, visit Hal Leonard online at
www.halleonard.com**

Prices, contents, and availability subject to change without notice.

RECORDED VERSIONS®

The Best Note-For-Note Transcriptions Available

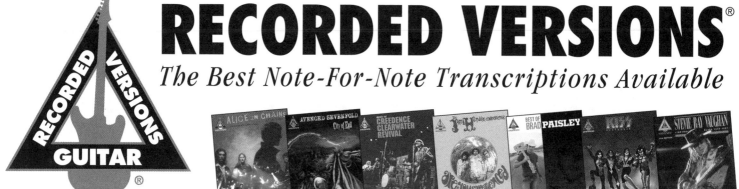

ALL BOOKS INCLUDE TABLATURE

14037551	AC/DC – Backtracks	$32.99
00692015	Aerosmith – Greatest Hits	$22.95
00690178	Alice in Chains – Acoustic	$19.95
00694865	Alice in Chains – Dirt	$19.95
00690812	All American Rejects – Move Along	$19.95
00690958	Duane Allman Guitar Anthology	$24.99
00694932	Allman Brothers Band – Volume 1	$24.95
00694933	Allman Brothers Band – Volume 2	$24.95
00694934	Allman Brothers Band – Volume 3	$24.95
00690865	Atreyu – A Deathgrip on Yesterday	$19.95
00690609	Audioslave	$19.95
00690820	Avenged Sevenfold – City of Evil	$24.95
00690366	Bad Company – Original Anthology	$19.95
00690503	Beach Boys – Very Best of	$19.95
00690489	Beatles – 1	$24.99
00694832	Beatles – For Acoustic Guitar	$22.99
00691014	Beatles Rock Band	$34.99
00690110	Beatles – White Album (Book 1)	$19.95
00691043	Jeff Beck – Wired	$19.99
00692385	Chuck Berry	$19.95
00690835	Billy Talent	$19.95
00690901	Best of Black Sabbath	$19.95
00690831	blink-182 – Greatest Hits	$19.95
00690913	Boston	$19.95
00690932	Boston – Don't Look Back	$19.99
00690491	David Bowie – Best of	$19.95
00690873	Breaking Benjamin – Phobia	$19.95
00690451	Jeff Buckley – Collection	$24.95
00690957	Bullet for My Valentine – Scream Aim Fire	$19.95
00691004	Chickenfoot	$22.99
00690590	Eric Clapton – Anthology	$29.95
00690415	Clapton Chronicles – Best of Eric Clapton	$18.95
00690936	Eric Clapton – Complete Clapton	$29.99
00690074	Eric Clapton – The Cream of Clapton	$24.95
00694869	Eric Clapton – Unplugged	$22.95
00690162	The Clash – Best of	$19.95
00690828	Coheed & Cambria – Good Apollo I'm Burning Star, IV, Vol. 1: From Fear Through the Eyes of Madness	$19.95
00690593	Coldplay – A Rush of Blood to the Head	$19.95
00690962	Coldplay – Viva La Vida	$19.95
00690819	Creedence Clearwater Revival – Best of	$22.95
00690648	The Very Best of Jim Croce	$19.95
00690613	Crosby, Stills & Nash – Best of	$22.95
00690967	Death Cab for Cutie – Narrow Stairs	$22.99
00690289	Deep Purple – Best of	$17.95
00690784	Def Leppard – Best of	$19.95
00692240	Bo Diddley	$19.99
00690347	The Doors – Anthology	$22.95
00690348	The Doors – Essential Guitar Collection	$16.95
00690810	Fall Out Boy – From Under the Cork Tree	$19.95
00690664	Fleetwood Mac – Best of	$19.95
00690870	Flyleaf	$19.95
00690931	Foo Fighters – Echoes, Silence, Patience & Grace	$19.95
00690808	Foo Fighters – In Your Honor	$19.95
00690805	Robben Ford – Best of	$19.95
00694920	Free – Best of	$19.95
00691050	Glee Guitar Collection	$19.99
00690848	Godsmack – IV	$19.95
00690943	The Goo Goo Dolls – Greatest Hits Volume 1: The Singles	$22.95
00701764	Guitar Tab White Pages – Play-Along	$39.99
00694854	Buddy Guy – Damn Right, I've Got the Blues	$19.95

00690840	Ben Harper – Both Sides of the Gun	$19.95
00694798	George Harrison – Anthology	$19.95
00690841	Scott Henderson – Blues Guitar Collection	$19.95
00692930	Jimi Hendrix – Are You Experienced?	$24.95
00692931	Jimi Hendrix – Axis: Bold As Love	$22.95
00692932	Jimi Hendrix – Electric Ladyland	$24.95
00690017	Jimi Hendrix – Live at Woodstock	$24.95
00690602	Jimi Hendrix – Smash Hits	$24.99
00690793	John Lee Hooker Anthology	$24.99
00690692	Billy Idol – Very Best of	$19.95
00690688	Incubus – A Crow Left of the Murder	$19.95
00690544	Incubus – Morningview	$19.95
00690790	Iron Maiden Anthology	$24.99
00690721	Jet – Get Born	$19.95
00690684	Jethro Tull – Aqualung	$19.95
00690959	John5 – Requiem	$22.95
00690814	John5 – Songs for Sanity	$19.95
00690751	John5 – Vertigo	$19.95
00690845	Eric Johnson – Bloom	$19.95
00690846	Jack Johnson and Friends – Sing-A-Longs and Lullabies for the Film Curious George	$19.95
00690271	Robert Johnson – New Transcriptions	$24.95
00699131	Janis Joplin – Best of	$19.95
00690427	Judas Priest – Best of	$22.99
00690742	The Killers – Hot Fuss	$19.95
00690975	Kings of Leon – Only by the Night	$22.99
00694903	Kiss – Best of	$24.95
00690355	Kiss – Destroyer	$16.95
00690834	Lamb of God – Ashes of the Wake	$19.95
00690875	Lamb of God – Sacrament	$19.95
00690823	Ray LaMontagne – Trouble	$19.95
00690679	John Lennon – Guitar Collection	$19.95
00690781	Linkin Park – Hybrid Theory	$22.95
00690743	Los Lonely Boys	$19.95
00690720	Lostprophets – Start Something	$19.95
00690955	Lynyrd Skynyrd – All-Time Greatest Hits	$19.99
00694954	Lynyrd Skynyrd – New Best of	$19.95
00690754	Marilyn Manson – Lest We Forget	$19.95
00694956	Bob Marley – Legend	$19.95
00694945	Bob Marley– Songs of Freedom	$24.95
00690657	Maroon5 – Songs About Jane	$19.95
00120080	Don McLean – Songbook	$19.95
00694951	Megadeth – Rust in Peace	$22.95
00690951	Megadeth – United Abominations	$22.99
00690505	John Mellencamp – Guitar Collection	$19.95
00690646	Pat Metheny – One Quiet Night	$19.95
00690558	Pat Metheny – Trio: 99>00	$19.95
00690040	Steve Miller Band – Young Hearts	$19.95
00694883	Nirvana – Nevermind	$19.95
00690026	Nirvana – Unplugged in New York	$19.95
00690807	The Offspring – Greatest Hits	$19.95
00694847	Ozzy Osbourne – Best of	$22.95
00690399	Ozzy Osbourne – Ozzman Cometh	$22.99
00690933	Best of Brad Paisley	$22.95
00690995	Brad Paisley – Play: The Guitar Album	$24.99
00690866	Panic! At the Disco – A Fever You Can't Sweat Out	$19.95
00690938	Christopher Parkening – Duets & Concertos	$24.99
00694855	Pearl Jam – Ten	$19.95
00690439	A Perfect Circle – Mer De Noms	$19.95
00690499	Tom Petty – Definitive Guitar Collection	$19.95
00690428	Pink Floyd – Dark Side of the Moon	$19.95
00690789	Poison – Best of	$19.95
00693864	The Police – Best of	$19.95

00694975	Queen – Greatest Hits	$24.95
00690670	Queensryche – Very Best of	$19.95
00690878	The Raconteurs – Broken Boy Soldiers	$19.95
00694910	Rage Against the Machine	$19.95
00690055	Red Hot Chili Peppers – Blood Sugar Sex Magik	$19.95
00690584	Red Hot Chili Peppers – By the Way	$19.95
00690852	Red Hot Chili Peppers –Stadium Arcadium	$24.95
00690511	Django Reinhardt – Definitive Collection	$19.95
00690779	Relient K – MMHMM	$19.95
00690631	Rolling Stones – Guitar Anthology	$27.95
00694976	Rolling Stones – Some Girls	$22.95
00690264	The Rolling Stones – Tattoo You	$19.95
00690685	David Lee Roth – Eat 'Em and Smile	$19.95
00690942	David Lee Roth and the Songs of Van Halen	$19.95
00690031	Santana's Greatest Hits	$19.95
00690566	Scorpions – Best of	$22.95
00690604	Bob Seger – Guitar Collection	$19.95
00690803	Kenny Wayne Shepherd Band – Best of	$19.95
00690968	Shinedown – The Sound of Madness	$22.99
00690813	Slayer – Guitar Collection	$19.95
00690733	Slipknot – Vol. 3 (The Subliminal Verses)	$22.99
00120004	Steely Dan – Best of	$24.95
00694921	Steppenwolf – Best of	$22.95
00690655	Mike Stern – Best of	$19.95
00690877	Stone Sour – Come What(ever) May	$19.95
00690520	Styx Guitar Collection	$19.95
00120081	Sublime	$19.95
00120122	Sublime – 40oz. to Freedom	$19.95
00690929	Sum 41 – Underclass Hero	$19.95
00690767	Switchfoot – The Beautiful Letdown	$19.95
00690993	Taylor Swift – Fearless	$22.99
00690830	System of a Down – Hypnotize	$19.95
00690799	System of a Down – Mezmerize	$19.95
00690531	System of a Down – Toxicity	$19.95
00694824	James Taylor – Best of	$16.95
00690871	Three Days Grace – One-X	$19.95
00690737	3 Doors Down – The Better Life	$22.95
00690683	Robin Trower – Bridge of Sighs	$19.95
00699191	U2 – Best of: 1980-1990	$19.95
00690732	U2 – Best of: 1990-2000	$19.95
00660137	Steve Vai – Passion & Warfare	$24.95
00690116	Stevie Ray Vaughan – Guitar Collection	$24.95
00660058	Stevie Ray Vaughan – Lightnin' Blues 1983-1987	$24.95
00694835	Stevie Ray Vaughan – The Sky Is Crying	$22.95
00690557	Stevie Ray Vaughan – Texas Flood	$19.95
00690772	Velvet Revolver – Contraband	$22.95
00690071	Weezer (The Blue Album)	$19.95
00690966	Weezer – (Red Album)	$19.99
00690447	The Who – Best of	$24.95
00690916	The Best of Dwight Yoakam	$19.95
00690905	Neil Young – Rust Never Sleeps	$19.99
00690623	Frank Zappa – Over-Nite Sensation	$22.99
00690589	ZZ Top Guitar Anthology	$24.95

Prices and availability subject to change without notice. Some products may not be available outside the U.S.A.

0211